GRAPHIC EXPEDITIONS

BUILDING THE GREAT WALL OF CHINA

AN Isabel Soto
HISTORY ADVENTURE

by Terry Collins
illustrated by Joe Staton and Al Milgrom

Consultant:
Dr. Hanchao Lu
Professor and Director of Graduate Studies
School of History, Technology, and Society
Georgia Institute of Technology
Atlanta, Georgia

Capstone
press

Mankato, Minnesota

Graphic Library is published by Capstone Press,
151 Good Counsel Drive, P.O. Box 669, Mankato, Minnesota 56002.
www.capstonepress.com

Books published by Capstone Press are manufactured with paper
containing at least 10 percent post-consumer waste.

Library of Congress Cataloging-in-Publication Data
Collins, Terry.
    Building the Great Wall of China: an Isabel Soto history adventure / by Terry Collins;
illustrated by Joe Staton and Al Milgrom.
    p. cm. — (Graphic library. Graphic expeditions)
    Summary: "In graphic novel format, follows the adventures of Isabel Soto as
she explores the history behind the building of the Great Wall of China" — Provided
by publisher.
    Includes bibliographical references and index.
    ISBN 978-1-4296-3411-3 (library binding)
    ISBN 978-1-4296-3890-6 (softcover)
    1. Great Wall of China (China) — History — Comic books, strips, etc. — Juvenile
literature. 2. Graphic novels. I. Staton, Joe, ill. II. Milgrom, Al, ill. III. Title. IV. Series.
DS793.G67C65 2010
951 — dc22   2009001171

Designer
Alison Thiele

Cover Artist
Tod G. Smith

Colorist
Krista Ward

Media Researcher
Wanda Winch

Editor
Christopher L. Harbo

Photo Credits: AP Images/Vincent Yu, 8; Shutterstock/Mikhail Nekrasov, 13

Design Elements: Shutterstock/Chen Ping Hung (framed edge design); mmmm (world map
design); Mushakesa (abstract lines design); Najin (old parchment design)

TABLE OF CONTENTS

Chisholm Trail, Texas, 1876

My grandfather used to say, "Isabel, people can learn a great deal from history."

I've been studying cattle drives for two days now. All I've learned is how it feels to be soaking wet.

I wish something interesting would happen.

BOOM!

STAMPEDE!

My grandfather also used to say, "Be careful what you wish for. It just might come true."

No time to program a destination into the W.I.S.P.

I'll just jump through the portal blindly!

THUD THUD THUD THUD

Where's my exit?

There! Straight ahead.

Wherever we end up, I just hope it isn't raining.

The Tumu Crisis of 1449 began when Zhu Qizhen was the sixth emperor of China's Ming Dynasty.

Tired of being invaded by Mongolia, he led his soldiers into a great battle.

However, the fight ended when the Mongols captured the emperor.

Meanwhile, Zhu Qizhen's brother Zhu Qiyu was named as the new emperor.

But with the Chinese Army defeated, how would China fight back?

THE MING DYNASTY

The Ming Dynasty began ruling China in 1368. The dynasty was founded when the Han Chinese overthrew the Yuan Dynasty. The Ming Dynasty's government lasted 276 years. During that time, Chinese literature, art, and philosophy grew. The dynasty came to an end in 1644 when the Qing Dynasty rose to power.

Zhu Qiyu's advisors recommended another kind of protection. For centuries, the Chinese had used walls to protect their cities and lands.

These primitive walls were old and worn.

They were incomplete and spread out across the northern Chinese border.

But a new "great" wall made of brick and stone could keep out the Mongol raiders.

This wall would be longer, taller, and stronger.

Other Great Wall Myths

What brings you to China, Dr. Soto?

Would you believe it had something to do with a cattle stampede?

Eddie? Now where has that boy gone?

Oh boy. I've got a pretty good idea.

CHECK THE MAP

GREAT WALL

BEIJING

The Great Wall of China is the longest structure on earth made by humans. It has several different sections. Depending on what part of China is visited, the wall may be either unbroken or in ruins. Vandals have damaged many parts of the wall. Other parts of the wall have been knocked down for new construction projects. People have even stolen bricks to build their own homes.

THE FIRST ROYAL EMPEROR OF CHINA

Emperor Shi Huangdi founded the Qin Dynasty and brought China together. Roads were built to connect the cities. A central government was put in place. The Chinese now used the same money, measures, and written language.

Stick close. I'll open another portal. I'm taking you back to your parents.

Come on. Let's jump!

Great Wall of China, 1642

Are we there yet?

No. The W.I.S.P. says we've arrived around the end of the Ming Dynasty.

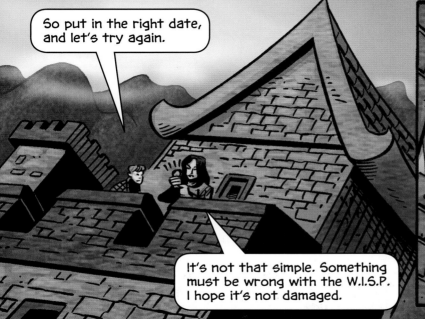

So put in the right date, and let's try again.

It's not that simple. Something must be wrong with the W.I.S.P. I hope it's not damaged.

Hold on, soldiers are coming.

Great Wall of China, present day

We made it!

THUMP!

Edward James Elliot! Your mother and I were worried sick!

I knew he would be safe with Dr. Soto watching him.

What's with the headgear?

Souvenir.

Are you all right, son?

I'm fine, but the Great Wall of China is awesome!

I never thought Eddie would be so excited about history. Thank you, Dr. Soto.

Firsthand knowledge is what hooked him, not me.

Eddie just needed to see with his own eyes what went into the building of the Great Wall.

I think we can all be glad that one of the world's most amazing building achievements is still standing.

Enjoy the rest of your stay in China, Eddie.

Don't worry, Dr. Soto. I will!

27

MORE ABOUT THE GREAT WALL

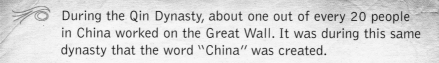

- During the Qin Dynasty, about one out of every 20 people in China worked on the Great Wall. It was during this same dynasty that the word "China" was created.

- Building the Great Wall was very expensive. To pay for the materials, the Chinese government raised taxes on the poor. This tax caused many citizens to dislike the wall.

- The average height of the Great Wall is 25 feet (8 meters). The width of the wall ranges from 15 to 25 feet (5 to 8 meters). Along most sections, a 13-foot- (4-meter-) wide roadway runs along the top of the wall.

- The Great Wall was built to defend China from raiders and other invaders. Today the wall serves as a popular tourist destination. Each year, more than 10 million tourists visit the Great Wall.

- The Badaling is one of the most visited sections of the Great Wall. This section was built during the Ming Dynasty. It is located about 43 miles (69 kilometers) north of China's capital of Beijing. The Badaling section is famous for the way the Great Wall snakes up and down mountain slopes.

- On June 25, 1899, a hoax appeared in newspapers across the United States. In this fake story, rumors flew about American businessmen planning to tear down the Great Wall. They would then build a road in its place to help the Chinese economy.

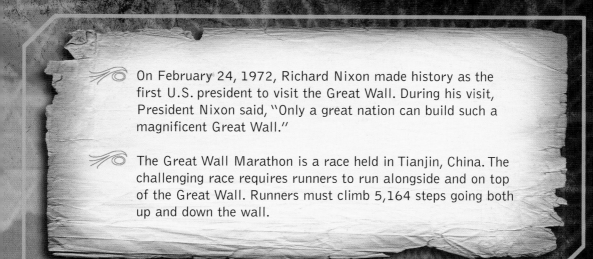

On February 24, 1972, Richard Nixon made history as the first U.S. president to visit the Great Wall. During his visit, President Nixon said, "Only a great nation can build such a magnificent Great Wall."

The Great Wall Marathon is a race held in Tianjin, China. The challenging race requires runners to run alongside and on top of the Great Wall. Runners must climb 5,164 steps going both up and down the wall.

MORE ABOUT

NAME: Dr. Isabel "Izzy" Soto
DEGREES: History and Anthropology
BUILD: Athletic   **HAIR:** Dark Brown
EYES: Brown   **HEIGHT:** 5' 7"

W.I.S.P.: The Worldwide Inter-dimensional Space/Time Portal developed by Max Axiom at Axiom Laboratory.

BACKSTORY: Dr. Isabel "Izzy" Soto caught the history bug as a little girl. Every night, her grandfather told her about his adventures exploring ancient ruins in South America. He believed lost cultures teach people a great deal about history.

Izzy's love of cultures followed her to college. She studied history and anthropology. On a research trip to Thailand, she discovered an ancient stone with mysterious energy. Izzy took the stone to Super Scientist Max Axiom, who determined that the stone's energy cuts across space and time. Harnessing the power of the stone, he built a device called the W.I.S.P. It opens windows to any place and any time. Izzy now travels through time to see history unfold before her eyes. Although she must not change history, she can observe and investigate historical events.

GLOSSARY

achievement (uh-CHEEV-muhnt) — a successful accomplishment, especially after a lot of effort

bamboo (bam-BOO) — a tropical grass with a hard, hollow stem

catapult (KAT-uh-puhlt) — a weapon used to hurl rocks, liquid, or other items at an enemy

crisis (KRYE-siss) — a time of danger or difficulty

dynasty (DYE-nuh-stee) — a series of rulers belonging to the same family or group

emperor (EM-pur-ur) — a male ruler of an empire; Chinese emperors made all the decisions for the people they ruled.

enthusiasm (en-THOO-zee-az-uhm) — great excitement or interest

myth (MITH) — a false idea that many people believe

peasant (PEZ-uhnt) — a poor person who owns a small farm or works on a farm, especially in Europe and some Asian countries

philosophy (fuh-LOSS-uh-fee) — the study of truth, wisdom, the nature of reality, and knowledge

primitive (PRIM-uh-tiv) — relating to an early stage of development

sorcery (SOR-sur-ee) — magic that controls evil spirits

stampede (stam-PEED) — when a group of animals makes a sudden, wild rush in one direction, usually because something has frightened them

READ MORE

Guillain, Charlotte. *Ancient China.* China Focus. Chicago: Heinemann Library, 2008.

Mah, Adeline Yen. *China: Land of Dragons and Emperors.* New York: Delacorte Press, 2009.

Morley, Jacqueline. *You Wouldn't Want to Work on the Great Wall of China!: Defenses You'd Rather Not Build.* New York: Franklin Watts, 2006.

O'Neill, Joseph R. *The Great Wall of China.* Essential Events. Edina, Minn.: ABDO, 2009.

Wilkinson, Philip. *Chinese Myth: A Treasury of Legends, Art, and History.* The World of Mythology. Armonk, N.Y.: Sharpe Focus, 2008.

INTERNET SITES

FactHound offers a safe, fun way to find Internet sites related to this book. All sites on FactHound have been researched by our staff.

Here's all you do:

Visit *www.facthound.com*

FactHound will fetch the best sites for you!

INDEX